Praise for
a "Working Life"

"Myles's poems chop lines into uncanny units and place our lexicons under an X-ray, turning the familiar into the unfamiliar. Myles evokes the absurd grace of mundane life—coffee, dog, toilet, ex-lover, refrigerator, T-shirt, cat, books, therapy, toaster—but among these quotidian objects and companions, there's always a spark of surprise, as the sharp philosophical lines stop us in our tracks." **—*The Guardian***

"Impressive . . . With just a few words per line, their poems move down the page quickly, the language dashed off and immediate, as though keeping pace with the poet's mind. Some feel like shorthand entries in a diary . . . [Reveals] the joys of a life built out of thinking, dreaming, and making." **—*Publishers Weekly***

"It is important to stay happy, to maintain daily reminders of goodness and wonder, and in *a 'Working Life'*, Eileen Myles helps us do just that. With their streamlined style and singular devotion to mundane wonder, they show how life can still be surprising despite the inevitability we may feel each day. Contradictions and coincidences, joy and despair, the intricacies of life and death are all captured in these brief, fleeting poems, told in tight verse and with some lines only a word long. They reflect how quickly time goes by and how each second provides something deep and new, creating an infinite loop of meaning—a message that is helpful and frustrating, uplifting and perplexing. Really, it's life." **—*BookPage***

Praise for
Eileen Myles

"Myles's poems set a bar for openness, frankness, and variability few lives could ever match . . . Now Myles is older than [Robert] Lowell when he died, and enjoying [their] greatest moment of accomplishment and fame. [Myles's] very presence in the world is a form of activism, but [their] work, when studied with care, is also political in the sense that it gives evidence of one of the richest and most conflicted human hearts you're likely to find."

—Dan Chiasson, *New York Review of Books*

"Choreography's calligraphic touch: Bill T. Jones, Jackson Pollock, Eileen Myles. [Myles] moves so generously, stays so lightly, has so openly found and crafted life, as ceremony, every day, it's as if [their] hands and feet trail sonic pigment, chromatic grammar, so that the earth is constantly refreshed by the poems as [they] step and caress, with ear's utmost care, as curate of our common experiment, our undercommon experience."   **—Fred Moten**

a
"Working
Life"

Also by Eileen Myles

a "Working Life"

Eileen Myles

Grove Press

New York

Published simultaneously in Canada
Printed in Canada

This book was set in 11-pt. Bembo
by Alpha Design & Composition of Pittsfield, NH.

First Grove Atlantic hardcover edition: April 2023
First Grove Atlantic paperback edition: April 2024

Library of Congress Cataloging-in-Publication data is available for this title.

ISBN 978-0-8021-6329-5
eISBN 978-0-8021-6190-1

Grove Press
an imprint of Grove Atlantic
154 West 14th Street
New York, NY 10011

Distributed by Publishers Group West

groveatlantic.com

24 25 26   10 9 8 7 6 5 4 3 2 1

for Fanny Howe

Contents

a
"Working Life"

For My Friend

Nothing
better
for people
than dogs
nothing better than ma
king
you scream
here. There were
two super
new cars
and then
some pink
chicken
filets
I guess
there were
berries
for sale
in Scandinavia
a man in
a plaid
shirt &
cookies
also they
are
working

in the ceme
tery
I can see
their blue
ladder
from here.
A man
has written
a book
about many
deaths
or many
things to do after.
Read it
read it
they say
but what
comes
after
is a small
idea. Now
is large
rainy.
Amy I wish
you luck

The Preface
some landscape for joan

My vanity
all kinds of roads

looking out
at the blue
black mountains
and so many
houses down
among the floor
the crime
of so many of us

big bold stripe
overhead
but it's
different
too
it's not how
the dinosaurs
saw

3

one volume
held what turned
out to
be the window
of my
life

I keep plunging

you just have
to wait

till it sees
you again

only that
one lens

to be
enough to the father
of the day

and her sound
it's layed
out so regular
like god

and you just
pick out
your business
and land
on the land

the stripes
the crawling
ants; look what we've
done

the other
window
darker pony
I'm such
a mess

finally seeing
the end of
it thank
god is always
the mountains
and that's
why we call
them friends

that's my limit

and here's the plane
now and the
town <u>bump</u>

Page America Myles

I have a land
line so in
a state of
emergency
I can make
a call.
 So you should
    get a
      landline
    so I can
    call you
    that's what
    I meant
to say to Erin.
there's a lot
of suffering
here in this
room. I meant

to connect to a therapist.

That's what
I planned
to do in

the city.
I'll do that
this week.
In that
case this
means
next. It's
like my
body's
pointing w
time full
of time.
That's
what I meant
to say
to you
let's have
some.

First Poem

every
experience
of being
& day
awakens
me to the dif
ficulty
I change
my socks
I see
my feet
you don't
so much
mind my flaws
I think
at the
world
when I
go out. women
in chairs
& couch
one of both
a tender

dog & actual
tears. today
it snows.
we go
live

Mary Queen of Scots

The whales
breaking
the surface
are the
ocean
no other
name. Then
I knew
that I
became
ocean
too. The black
and white
mother
knows her
baby becomes
knives
she misses
the restaur
ant. And
honey
runs out
and takes
a bite

of Butters'
head
the owner
is nice
that forest
in Scotland
whipping
by. Yes I
think this
country
should
become
free. Solaris
is the
interior
of my sexual
fantasies
I'm part
plant
eaten
by movies
for years
the veal
of snow
curves
as she drags
her pile
of trash
on the train

this is
any
butter
the lightly
screaming
train &
I'm excited
to see
you. Black
barns
hold my
content
ment. Dana
Ward and
Mira
Gonzalez
and those
small tubby
rolls
in the grass
are relevant
yellower
grass. It's
hay. Hedge
ends
the property
my this
is not
struck

by the gun
of a moment
but this
tumbling
green
long unseen
tiny recollections
exchanging
thwang
the release
of a bow. Honey's
safe and
butters
safe. The crown
of a tree
see through
poking
over a hill
and I
want
my hands
on the font
I want
I want

Friday Night

I don't think
I can
live without
taking pic
tures. The peach
second
sun made
a move
on the right.
No clouds
shifted
in realistic
terms
made
that melon
bright. But
what
about the
singular
spray
of leaves
that made
me think
of sight

no see
an open
space
& a hook
a beck
oning
space
that
shakes
when
there's
wind
what's
the heart
but an
emptiness
in your
stomach
a hole
in your
head
a foot
on the
bed
you happy
you made
me happy
non understandable
us like

nature
unknown
all fronds
all silence
sound
pulling
the trigger
always.

In You

I feel very
protective
of wood
if it's
living
you can rain
on it
but in the
sink
it rots
so love it
like a baby
worship
the tree.
Love the lightbulb
in many
colors
the blond
for her
brightness
forgive
me for the
obvious
my love

deep & translucent
troubled
the candle
love the candle
for its powerful
tongue
the dog
for his
breath
whatever
sex
politeness
brings
me much.
I plan
for your
death
mine is
the end
of the
poem
it must be
long
to direct
to multiply
steam &
explode
love the fork
its tines

are how
I want to
be invaluable
silly name.
Love Texas
like a dog
in a hat.
this makes
my poetry
rise. Replace
it with
heat
keel towards
me please
be present
I wrote on
you
I write with
you. I sleep
on you
hold my
love, steam
my flight
bury me
deep
I am one
of you
loving
you well &

the shame
that brought
us here
I write
a big
apology
in one
lifetime
I do little
open ended
at my
best. Thank
you for
your time.
For this
long wet-
ting.

To Love

Do you
only
go to new
places
is it true
did the
planet
just get
born

you in your
little legs
and I
am in my
tree
am love
the baby
crying is
the bouncing
plane
the strange
wind
that killed
Bob

all of it
is true
and I in
my rot
am having
the
time
of my
life.

Russia

I read
a book &
then I want
to read
another
one about
Russia
about the bath
tub. I think
Russia's
too much
like me dry
& cruel. Blue
wild cerebral
dour. The poets
there have
been brain
washed
by the
team
of white
poets
preceding
me

who ex
plained
that in
america
everything's
confessional
except
them. My
intention
was to
muddle
through my
reading
not <u>mud</u>
dle but
wander
explain
how I
like a mind
like a spaciousness
that hungers
for more
and can
get lost
inside
your there
ness
for days

Tasha

She prefers
my phone &

using my
computer
w out the burden
of her life
last night
I described
it open
a circle
she kisses
my knee
its life
that is
my name
they thought
she had
a lot
I think
it's enough
I mean
it's astonishing
if I had (his)

I could
feel everything
but as it is
I know
what it is
I love your
lips.

Casper

This is not the end of the story oh no
I may begin my life as a college student approximately

88 miles from the US Mexico
border here on the white

steps of Sul Ross University named after a confederate
   general.
Here if they accept me I may study thought

and meaning and study
itself, I may study plankton and clouds, mountains
cell phones and ghosts.
But I am a ghost
born in Eileen's child
hands head of paper
mache, a gown fashioned
of soft cloth that Emma found. In a way a puppet, a
   ghost truth
be told is a zombie, the undead. Never born
never dying. Never arriving.

I make common cause now
with the slaves of the world, prisoners of our security
state, and most abundantly
most locally today, America's prisoners of war,

not immigrants, illegals, aliens, but refugees—children
women and men in
jails and cages not far from here. A multitude, less visible
than a ghost,
more silent than a puppet.
They are not criminals
these people brayed about by politicians, held away from
friendship, pleasure, health and safety in the dark
but refugees in a never ending war this country wages
against
the poor and
vulnerable, victims, descendants, recipients of our endless
interventions
in Latin America, our wars, world-wide, and in our jails
detained at our borders,
helped by our friend Israel exporting their security kraft
around the world. Abolish all of it, the borders and the
jails
and the police
state, open the door, R.I.P.
not rest in peace, but abolish the racist imperialist
patriarchy, abolish it abolish it

abolish it

abolish it

abolish it

abolish it

Now.

Read

skiers
miss the
snow &
scientists
notice that
what they're
studying
is gone. Study
gone. Caroline
says the mountains
will be
out & Justin
said I was
funny. I push
the christmassy
door. When
I run out
of my poem
I will write
the poem
you gave
me. Enough
poems enough

dogs. Making
is just taking if
you know. Knew.
doo-doo doo

September 7

The vagina of my life
is so stretched
out. I thought
where am i
hundreds of my students
landed in Brooklyn
like we did last week
but it was another
church. I saw the fear
in their faces
as I was climbing
the gates and demanding
we make
the next connection
it was an old church
the congregation
was various ecstatic
yes that's what
this is a little
crazy lost poor
everyone they needed
an assignment. When
did we last me[e]t
when do we

meet again
is this just sentimental
am I the priest
describe the congregation
that's what I'll ask
it was a little
like Qalandia
the churches were
trains, they were
nations, homeless
they were punishment
we seemed to gather
here. Describe
us that's the only
hope. Why are
we out, why aren't
we home, no it's us
and I know
you very well
you seem to be
following me, I brought
you here, what
do I want. It's city-less
it's godless, it's fatherless
it's motherless it
always feels the
same meeting at monuments
god asking for something
maybe. I lost my

notebook, my computer
died, I smell like
fear, I didn't get any
sleep. I wanted
to be here. I couldn't
keep watching that
show, I finished
the book about
trees. Everything's stone
in the name of god
but it's just us, pointless
at night, I'm not
really at the helm, I
can't be blamed, did
I ask you here, I just
woke up like
everyone in this
swarm, it's my disease
that I think
I'm responsible, that it's
a class, it's not
a reading, I'm not
in charge. I said
over there. Think
Think, give them a pur-
pose, why did you
come here tonight, tell
me what you see,

tell me who we are
what we want. Come
back here again, next week
or sometime
Show me what you
did. Only the
shrink asked
if I said this to every-
one. What did I
say. Am I saying
it now. Is that
why we're here. Tell
me next week, next
month, next year.
I'll send a mailing
Tomorrow. You'll know
when to come. I'll
know who you are
I won't forget
anyone. If I
seemed like I would
always be there
well it just
isn't true. You know
at a certain
point you hate
the theme song
but you have

to go on. This
is after that.
This is next. What
did he like. I
guess everyone's
asking you that
now. What do I
like. All of us
out there at night
not even looking
for god. Looking for religion.
Not even that. Looking
at churches. Meeting
there. Looking
back. To see what
I want. You can
make me choose.
It's not that I have
a purpose. It's more
like I don't want
you to think I don't
have one. It's not
that I don't have
sex. Don't like it.
I forget where
It happens. I can
fix that. I can
start while I

travel. Just having
a little bit
with everyone. The next
time I see you
all

Did you indeed
dance under
a tree
with
goats
In the dark

Lucky Kittens

I met something
cool and I can't
shake it.
I want to write
a poem
to the new
thing. Nothing
more trans
than taking
a shit in the men's
room in
a hotel.
Also I
had a perfect
break
fast
and am well.
I exercised.
All good
things.
And once again
I'm flying.

A world
without mother
is a world
without
meat. I'm not crying
I'm flying
Honestly
I took
my mother's tear
from the
corner
of her
eye. It happened
when she
died.

I took
it on my
finger
and I wiped
it on
my jeans

The rattling
of paper
is an exquisite
dis
connect

old fashioned

all breaks

making space

always ready
for a fight

my heat is instantly
shadowy
like a moving
hand
or sound
like no jazz
at all

The Trip

I shall miss you. Drinking
grass like
that; a creature
drinks
from a stream
its time
& they feel
their own trickle
and warmth
and wonder
what's that
to know

my own
hug some
how the
language
slipping
the moon
drink
twice
once in my throat

and once
in my eyes
it's a new
year

How about it
is sleep better
than death
is day better
than night
is love better
than eternity
are dogs
better than
cats
is coffee
what is coffee
any groaning
machine
better than
any chirping
animal
is a child
better than a
building
is an unseeing
woman
better than not
is heat

better than
ice cold
day
bright day
better
than telling
the truth
is truth
the ugly
thing you
share
is sharing
beautiful
or hurtful
and cruel
does a pen
have words
in any
event
endless
are words
like bullets
tearing flesh
announcing
themselves
what do they
tell do hurtful
words tell
the end of something

the body al
ways cold
the day was
never new
life is a prison
how are you
drinking that
saying that
writing that
the puppets
groan
the heating
clanks
its OPEN
to you
a box or a vista
a plate of cheeeeese

Again

I'm just
doing
everything
all over
again
drinking
coffee
and being
alone
holding my pic
tures
gong she
goes
as the water
boils
forces
shushing
coming
to a close. Too fast
this winter
sings
holds

me fast
tuts
this winter's
sweet
enveloping or no?
there she
is. Something
dark
at last.

Notes

The road strikes
on moving
water.

Mike
KNOWS.

Mt
right
at the
end
of this

street

it was
a lease
but I
began to
have a
relationship
w this
car

Pigs

It is the first
day of the new
Year. The city honors
This day by not
Requiring us
To move our
Cars. I ran down
In flip flops
Then I looked
At the app
And discovered this
Fact. I sd
Hi to my neighbor
and stumbled
Up the stairs. Are you okay
she said. Yes
I said but I felt
Not ashamed but mussed
Rattled. I started reading the
New Yorker
Which seems so
In between

I said so on Twitter
And one woman started flirting
With me. I had showed
My address in a photo
Of the magazine
& it sounded like
She would be right
Over. I said I had six
Kids & my husband
Was a brute. My friend
In Chicago laughed.

Everything

The pizza shop had a bottle labeled
everything so delightedly
I shook it on my pizza
and jumped into
a cab. I'm old school New Yorker
I told Adam
I like the inexactness
of cabs, the cash
the entire ana
log experience
of them. The details
of the Joe & Charlie
visit is fading, I told
him about lunch
with Gail (but
not everything) the quote
she gave me I used
in our conversation in chairs
in front of people
was perfect is this. Here it is
la chance dans la mal chance
and by now sirens

is that the exact act of goodness
in life is often situated in the
bad the wrong the pizza
no longer warm by the time
I get home but Adam
I have to get off so now
I can eat it and I remember
the cold coffee in the refriger
ator that's where
the travelling mug
is I open the door
and then I close it
to sleep you have
to stop that stuff
some time and my toe throbs
from dropping the kryptonite
lock on it and I am not
going to Europe yes I am
I am going to London
next week so quaint and
dark not like us
and that is where
the good chance
is in the bad forcing the
thought to camp
and finish the slice
like Frank or
Charles bu
kowski

March 3

The quick
exchange
of emails
between
the former
lovers creates
a soft hole
in the day
and the
night
before. It snowed
but it was
supposed
to be larger &
everything's
closed the streets
are wet
I hear and I
won't
step into
them.

One poem
for today

but no
many little
ones. The coffee
slightly
altered
is good
my bare
feet in
bed ready
to work.
I work
in the field
of dreams
where I
have met
you many
times. I feel
closer, to
you this
morning
and probably
last night
when the
doorway
slightly
opened
because
of our

notes
was flooded
with ghosts.

When I was
young
I liked the
emptiness
of my
home &
now like
it or not
here is
this sweet
accumulation.

The cameras
all that
everything
I do can't
touch
the single
statement
of breeze &
loss & quaint
beauty
things I've
had since

I was a
kid
the secrets
of my home.
I feel con
demned
by this
chaotic
museum
of stuff &
yes I
desire
to photograph
it the
bowls u liked
the cup
u touched
& me in a teeshirt
that used
to be special
& now I
carouse in
bed w myself
in it. I don't
know if
this
will ever
be different
and that

is the
feeling of
this.

I feel like
a tree
the invisible
part of friendship
and drinking
together
and warning.

One empty wall
is the least
I can do
for myself.
Late at night
I enjoy
the brown
pages of a cowboy
show
teevee
on my lap
till practically
dawn
interesting
written
by a gambler

oh I have
so many
shows
one in Florence
one day
you were
taking a shower
I think
I thought
I love
this television

because
it's become
the way
to love
the road
of becoming
is a screen
belonging
on it in
my dream.

The excellent
moments
the man
barges in
and says
do you ever

think
about
film. The poetry
of accident
haunts
like a circus
tent over
my days

and that
fades
and a new
one. I
begin to
write
about dying.
THIS
story ends.
It begins
to be part
of the plot
and do I
love you
for your
distance
from it
or could
I love you
because

you are
close
or your
exciting
difference
so smart.
I love
myself.
The squeaky
little voice
that says
in here
owning the void
and grooving
on it. Voice
over
you're not
so bad
and then
I begin
to work.

My dead
mother
is around
my lover
not far
keeping u
here by

not calling
anyone
is that the tub
in which
I die.

Weir-doo
woo woo
woo

what's that
bird.

because
I don't
have kids
and this
is such
a blessing.

April 15

At the
very least

I expect
my next

cup of coffee
to be on
its way

and I can
hear it

the world
without
coffee
I expect
as a
kind of
rebirth

but I might
take

this borning
to the
end
in the way
I imagine
bed every
day dying

a good
dying & I

push my
coffee

against it
hello
each day

I like
day &
I thank death
for my
past &
future

every day
from
my toilet

I can
see it

winter wide
open
under
my bed.

And I'm
dying
to close
just that

I'm disabled
like

everyone
by climate

change

instead
getting
dithyram
bic

about
it choosing
this pen

import
that and
the constant
cheep
out my win
dow okay
okay
& the
trucks

when I
see
metaphors
I think
everything

when I
think
dithyramb
I dance

and ontology
is just
a belly

button

and then
I climb
out of
the fort

what plane
am I
on.   My

couch

you dirty
slave

the word
is political
even or especially

referring
to fur
niture

a caste
that comes &
goes
slowly
& builds
nothing

what on earth

running my
life at
all times

on a dirty
couch

pizza
in the park
w your
gleaming

intelligence

I think
of her

I cannot
resist

so what
is yur
smart
ness &

beauty
doing
for fun?

what is
the non
oppressive
condition
of love &
sex am I
even

interested
in doing
it squealing

on my
perch

or us singing
together

I hold
a candle

over you
& you
let me
in

when one is
letting
the other
come u
do feel
like the
great
liberator

man w
a lamp

the last two
lovers
I would
have to say

were not
interested
in who I
am

But
what am
I

That's the
puzzle

sitting
with
my pile
in this drift

bare legs

c'mon
in.

what is
that

a drill
next
door kind
of sweet

while I am
rearing

and the
green

leaves bobbing
out there
in the

light

my friend
outside

an ex
lover
walking around

I'm holding
the line

for this

dithyrambic
explosion

of morning
& everything

meeting

for one

the birds

deep *yes*

evolution

any
babies

why yes

always

enthusiastic

that they
go wide

wide
wide

unlike

that drill

Por Example

I will
sleep
on the ground
with the
wagon train
No I will
not. I
will make
a home.

gentle sucking
of the
faucet
& the wind
outside

Beloved Train

vampires cry blood

each poet
is required
before the time
of their
death
to stay up and
write
a vampire
novel. Even

though the
light doth

Kill them.
Day light
kills
vampires.
As you know.

It will be
a short novel.

I desired
to burn
like Joan
of Arc
being
woman man
saintly
and the
flames
made me
be something
magnific
ent. And

What was
the story?
A novel
requires
a novel
a hall
a corridor
a prismatic
corridor
human bodies
are coming
down
while being
alive
which we

the dead
watch. The candle
the human
lights
is a tiny
bell to the vampire
he comes
one night
and puts
his cold
hand
in my
mouth
and demand
that I
stop
changing so
he can
get his
story out.
a dog pushes
against
the thing
in which
I emboss
the book
glinting
and the ancient
word 'boss'

a strange
globe
from which
spin forth
the armaments
of the vam
pires
pain
his long life
his very
long life
warrior
once
housewife
next
pad on a dog's
toe, sore
another
time
maritime
always getting
licked. The
dog putting
her damp
paw onto the ground
in the
night
before the
day in

which the vampire
was born
I mean
he died.
I have
failed
in my task
of writing
my vampire
novel. I will
never try
again
but in the time
of a global
pandemic
rules
have changed
no more
essay portion
of SATs

no more
this
no more
this
no more
this

Göteborg

for Daphne & Alice

Came home and lost
tons of conscious
ness.

For a time I
stole trays
from hotels
& now I steal
cups

There was this towel
I really wanted.
Sweden *knows*
towels

There was a shirt
at the airport
white, sort
of flocked
mine in every
way except

for this
girth

I bought
the girth
a burger &
nearly missed
my plane.

I ran
and my heart
pounded

I was not so
fast

There was
a man
running with me

I yelled
36
in camaraderie

but he ignored
me but then

he started
dropping

shit. I've
been
there.

There's so much
coffee

There's plenty
of coffee

I wish
someone

was here.

I'm becoming
so sensitive

a person
who has
slept ten

hours
I'm like

Vincent Price
in anything

my soft voice
whispering
anything

There was
a woman
in my poem

no I mean
my dream

and she looked
like someone
I'd dated

before
no she
felt like
her

like she was
going to be

her
and it was
an intense
time
in both
of our lives

she was
finishing
something
and I was
making a
mountain
of sleep

it was
possibly
crazy
and she was
humoring
me but

I felt
our gap

about to
be closed

it must
be true

I thought
it feels

This way
the two
someones
about to become
us

This geological
drama

tons of
time manifest
like persons

I was
slowly
heaving my
self

forward
to close
the small

distance

and I was
struck
in the dream

by the fact
she was
anyone

and I do
this

make
her mine
to share

my coffee
it is
better
now

students!

the coffee
is good
it has
become right

for me
in the
day

and this
is the relationship
I wanted

the dark
liquid
waking me up
in a
stolen
cup

Jason Throws a Bolt

Ten men
on the
side of a moun
tain
dog trying
to make
a date
white snails
desperately
clinging to
the side
of the
land.
Jason
picking
brown
trees – No,
flowery
funky
brown
daisies
all the
walkers
in natural

tones
no neon

peach
sky
blue
sea
so what
approximation
a poem
from Greece
Apollo's
legs on
fat &
far. Com
municate
that
to a dog.
5 boats!
dog road
trimming
a mountain
of black
wormy
negotiation
plunging
to the
sea. There's
the wi fi

that funny
bird
write
tonight
I'm that
part
of nature
that doesn't
know
it so
well. Leave
it to
men. Picking
things. I
love breeze
Nature is
big I
feel scrawny

Mountain 3 boats

Dog
blocking
two.

The Library

Penny & Paisley study maps

Penny & Paisley abhor literature

Penny & Paisley wear hats

Paisley's got a bushy foot

wavy back

Penny's very thirsty

camping over the bowl

o'er the water like

a platypus. Just like that.

Like literature.

Like a library.

She's a beautiful mass.

She just sits there.

Paisley lifts her telescope.

At the acropolis. At the bay.

Ears are lost in her brownness.

Wiggle wave. Huff. Huff.

Penny & Paisley at the deli.

Three paradise please. Three

seasoned sausage and egg.

I love ruins says Penny.

Just get the sandwiches says Paisley.

Remember the dead. Every mountain in Greece

is named after Saint Elias. Remember him.

Get me sandwich. Day. Bay.

My breathing is like the chug
of a train. Forward always says Penny.

Lobby in lobby out. Get me a boat.

Penny & Paisley are sailing.

Dusk falling on the ruins, on Shelter island

on the sea. Penny & Paisley are singing.

As the light falls, as the sandwich warm

on the deck of the boat, as the dogs dive

in and splash around, and they're turning

to see what you see at sea

they sing

and the sun warms the dog

and the dog warms the egg

and the egg warms the sea

and the sea warms the day

Penny and Paisley are sailing

as they're swaying down the street

and the dogs wrote a book

and the dogs went to bed

and the dogs had a day

that's just what it said.

For Charles

Once in Wellfleet
we were
standing
up to our
waists
in water
Susan
was there
inside
the house
Emma
too

Felix I think
wasn't there
anyhow
I remember
then
I felt our
friendship
begin.

Go

My car gets off
on it
self it doesn't use
so much gas
my face grows no
hair grows
angry if
u call me
lady. Call me
music fish
light cloud
I'm going
good; tree top
pen I sprout
kiss
forgiveness
is everything
I grow old and hairy

pick me up
& carry

me I'm every
thing I sing

I'm 70

Bednewton

was
there EVER such
a woman in Poland
or a man who brought
those candies
to her bed
to her bed

in film
without conscious
ness. And there was still
that tear

the cold that is making them cry
all the time
all his films were strung

together tonight for three hours
completely in film his film

The corpse of the man
Anne saw his body
Very beautiful

She said the dead look young
And rested

I walked up introduced
myself a little proud
white nobody
I think a person becomes
more general
a man proud to be any
man in order to
be feminist
and not hating her death
till the end
and I have more places
to put things
now she probably meant
in the state of no
relationship though I saw her
dash

I thought you
Were legit
He said
And he meant class
And she said it was
Cute Joan would
Have liked that women were the people I
most likely
corrected

about pronouns
was something
you wldn't catch men
each floor was like
a funeral home
rolling the cadavers
out daily of the rich
and they had to take
the freight elevator
of all the affront
of course he lived
Here
I become better – <u>worse</u>
He said
To be more like
My friends
And it didn't finally
Work.
She didn't go to any
readings
Any
more
she's dead like him
I went cause of the poetry
Connection
Inhale the nothing

that word
they said

Make it
Bigger

I figured he had
It in the family
In two of his films
He had one gotta be right
She said okay
We are so famous in
That poem
Throw it right at the building
I love that they had sex
that's right
Throw your damn poem
    bloody red scarf

Just like you think and that
Secret language
in here you're like a clown that
squeezing the long internal history
of women
emptying that song
and this is like a screen
cross-play a strong young question
stand up and say it
brings the inside out
Is there any translation with
out relation
ship

she said I live right around the corner
don't kill me
and he was like a prop
rugged handsome polish man
he was just feeling all that time
Should I shoot it. whatever was right.
into me or not it's just not making
me sad something is

yes, ship

she would sit there on the phone
being polish
for hours
it's all polish right
so many miles away
tears ran down
her face
being mum
you have me now
mother
have a big manhattan
<u>mom</u>
but she wanted
a son

WTF

when el presidente
mocks the
disabled
journalist
     'n gives
the female astronaut
the finger
it's not luck

the year is named
2020 for a rea
son. And we
have to make
up what it
is. It's not unusual
that I'm here
with you
I took last year off

I'm back
are you back
did you
know that Duterte

is supported
by the Marcos
family. Imelda Mar
cos is back
that tree
out the window
is. I'm
going to
have sex
in a really
good way. Today's
back. I'm offering
a simplistic
pattern for revolution
the necessary
return of
the conditions
hearing you pour
close & putting
it back in the ref
rigerator beep
the return to
love. The lamb
named Boris
saw an opening

in attaching
himself
to a warm

person who
he followed
around
and she asked
the farmer
can I take
him home

farmer sd
yes
Boris was
saved from
predictable
slaughter. Can
we save ourselves

every cow
that jumps
off the truck
can be free
will you
jump
with me. I have
picked someone
warm and she is sitting
on the couch

the flames
lick high

I am stoned
by the numbers
of this year

12 2020
2 2 2020
2 20 2020

plenty for you
plenty for me

I relax the slats
allowing in a
strip-ed light

flames
licking wildly

she's cooking a book
it's cooking wood

here's her beloved
foot. I have

followed someone
warm and look

where it took

me. I'm thinking

how funny the yeats
line on his
tombstone

horseman pass by

there are no horsemen

he imagined
futurity as antiquity

I do now.

the wildness
of the branches

out there. Some kind

of speech.

I doubt if this
is art

or labor or
an advice
column

I'm not lucky

you read
a lot of
books &

then you're
a sieve

once upon

a time I heard
poetry

nothing else was
catching
the words

in the air

I do

this

and the world
burns

I may be used
be burning alive

as the log falls

and knowing
that we
fall

turning

what ever
it means
but we
must

this land
is not
my land
it never
was
this is not high
school
where the
bullies
rule this
is the
future
or the
earth
no battle
it is/was

we're more
than enough

right

to turn
the blue
earth

to take
it home

the motion
is ours

jihad

There was a lunar
eclipse
in cancer
today

perhaps this is the
start
of the latest
in my new
breed
of very
bad poems

rangy
leggy

is this the night
of the
apocalypse

David's blue
lights

over
there

I don't
want
any lang
uage
to escape
me. the tower
against
the sky
and a better
guy than
me walking
his dog

my truck
makes
a funny
twirling
sound

turn the
corner
who am
I

at that
big
blaring
moon

the one
that stays
in
that reads
stop sign
one red
two white
two more
reds
dots
really
and the mountains
are here
dark
over
there
invisible

my dog
soignée
in bed

I ask her
please

the heat
here
falling
like
a kitten

in a period
that's
novelesque
it just
holds
all
of this
living

are you
writing
a book
or are
you just

in your
house

the wind
laughing
out there

even the
barcode
say resembles
the sky & the
sea
pat de groot's

bobbing
vision

& I wish
I bought
you when

mirrors
stretch
the light
a little
bit

longer
even multiply
light
bulbs

a lid
rolls
a re

flection

of power

a night
of tiny
things

homey
moons

will Masha
tell

how they did
it

the
boys
who
blew

up Bos
ton

looking
for great
ness

but it's
just a
spray
of salt

lime
in time

the surface
of a table
covered
with
book

open ladling
their
knowledge
to a non
reading

pile of
things

other books
compared

receipts

I don't
know
why electricity

reminds
me of

my mother
before the world
was language

and it only
was att
ached

to her

and the room
wasn't
everything
was
so she owns
the tingle

now of language
past

maybe now
when I
stay in

to be
alone with

my mother

new
dark
superstar

when she's

gone
and the
world's

full
of holes

and this
is it

I tell
my love

I just
want to live
in my hole

& it's
not even

language

now

I love
the train

her wide
whine

the whole
damn

world
is her

her sign

my mother
or my
lover

there's

not enough
of me

but
I'm sit
ting

here
to listen

warm
to be
in from
the cold

crack

says

the heat
(man)
did you
hear
that

I was
saying
that I

felt
nothing

and now
I al
ways

want to tell
you of
my world

you become
in your

life her

recording
device

her ears

and nose

her recording
clock

I couldn't
tell

her a thing

the insult
was

so great

she had
left

this
thing

that was
mine

a suit
of clothes

brain

only good

for recognizing

the unfathomable
sound

of the earth
being pounded

and producing
wind

or is it
my voice?

Howl

a refrigerator
makes a lot
of sound
so does a bird
people are
always talking
full of love
& pain
we started
a fund
and the dogs
are needing
some money &
I don't know
how to do
it & I'll
learn from
one of them
Tom's blue
shirt & glasses
are perfect.
My teeshirt

is good
my pen
works
I breathe.

we

we'll feed
you until
we kill
you but if
we leave

we won't
feed
you

light
in the
rain &
the rain's
pulsing

four
dark
little
steps

could
that be a
poodle

a dirty

old poodle
that's hungry

that poodle
could
be young
since
hunger is a great

e-
qualizer.

I had faith and confidence
and here we are

as a
child I was
inclined to
mas
turbation and
nose
picking

the movie's so
slow when they
sleep I want to
sleep

so I don't get
to bark

no you
don't
the new life:

½ the day
eating
½ the day
exercising

the dog's
their old roommate

this big
country

his big
country
bottle
is woven

the ordeal
of life:

funnels

and his

Macbeth

what re
mains is
a ½ hour

and it's
gonna be
a ½ hour

in so many
ways

Cool & Bright

I stand
up as I do

in my
poet's
shack &
piss
the toilet's
black.
An orange
moth
does its
last couple
of flaps
flap flap
pissed
to death
It could
be no
worse.
you flew.

Put My House

Put my house
inside the
boat

Can we do
that

put my dog
inside
of your
dog

put these birds
inside of
yours

put my ocean

put your ocean
all over
my mountains

put my mountains
in there

put my dog
in yours

my dog walk
is safe
inside your
dog walk

let me
eat inside
you. Let

me eat
your food

let me eat
your house

put your house
inside my
dog

put your dog
on my
boat

naturalize

put my heart
in yours

put my mouth
on your
mouth

put my hair
in yours

let me breathe
inside you

let me smell

your guts

put your boat
in my eye

let me eat
your friends

put these hours
inside your
hours

eat this bird
cheep

eat my
dog's
foot

eat that ocean

run to him
o'er the
o-o-cean

run to them
hear these
birds cheap

fly to me
eat my foot

put my house
inside yours
in your
mind think
me fly

this fly
me home
love me
now

forget your phone
eat my heart

run to him
o'er the o-o-cean

tweet tweet
tweet

dog growl

cluck

click

put my house

right in

there. Yeah

that's me
lookin out

the window

look at

me

bark bark
bark

put your heart
inside

that bark

Love Song

The sky hates me
I must be calm
I must be calm
if I have any
chance of good
            ness

at all
a child in
a snowstorm
a man faces
death
slow

a gibbet
is hanging
I don't
know what
it is

for a few
dollars

I can save
a horse

a deer
must hide

my dog
is far away
your dog

a joker
is close

a man travels
with
a wolf
& that is Victor
Hugo

his inkiness
is pure

translation
perhaps

I have
charm
in my
native
language

shelves
pushed up

against
each
other to
jam
the door

flinging
it open
I am

terribly
in love
with you

I cite
your gifts

I suggest
I am best
without
you and yet

this yellow
wind
I saw
the day

you were
there
and I never
felt such
desire

I say
I am
in decline

how could
you possibly

want <u>this</u>

alone
I'm strong

alone
I'm a muffin

I offer
you a

piece
of my
charm

and relinquish

my attachment
to being
a hermit

in an
old
wooden

house
I am kindly

to your
child

he is
ours.

Time Today

I sit down
to tie
my sneakers
and Honey
floods &
flows
to my other
side

I'm unwrapping
time
today
no I'm re
wrapping it.

It's been loosed
& I need
strictures

back cause
fear is out

there in
its ambling
tooth

Because I Was In

a pig stepped
up to the
mike & said
save me

the refrigerator
door said
hello

Erin zoomed
I changed
my shirt

the filter
wouldn't
fold

I said
what's going
on

he said
it's Chinese
it comes

from
China

I sd you're
not my
president

but neither
is she

the mango
is soft today

& it doesn't
matter what
cup I used

I wrote xxx ooo xxx
ooo xxx ooo xxx ooo
xxx ooo xxx ooo xxx

ooo I wrote xxx ooo xxx
ooo xxx ooo xxx ooo

and I could've gone
on forever

she wouldn't finish
the scrabble game

cause she needed
to sleep

the connection in
my town is so
slow she'd make

her move & I'd wait

            to see it

I mean that's why

she got sleepy

I mean say

it simply

say it

maybe therapy

can fit right

here. I mean

all of it.

the sound of her

body means

she's waiting

for the sound

of her food

on the floor

& I'm the chef

cause I open

a can. I hear

her crunchy

chewy good morning

David you're
my man

Joe & Charlie
are staying in

Sophie's sick

& that's why she's
needy. When she's
better she says
she'll enjoy the
pleasures of
isolation

I guess cause
I was getting
wiggy

my dog says
I'm thinking
of going back
to bed

I say fine
I'm going
to do therapy

she's still cleaning
her mouth
in the kitchen

she does it while
she thinks

considering
her move

and a bird outside
tweets

they can pay
me for the first
500 words
but it seems
I'm on
a slide

of staying in

it began
when the pig
spoke

previously I'd
been in Colombia
trying to pick
my clothes
but eileen doesn't
travel any more

she goes lap lap
lap

I don't know
what u should
do a bird
goes tweet

she sniffs
my sweat shirt

you were looking
very good on
Instagram yesterday

you have no idea

even sharpening
a pencil
is a pleasure

have you tried
it

and now I
think I'll
pee

her shadow
follows me

she does down
ward dog

I pee

she sneezes

maybe I'll eat

before therapy

she looks
beautiful sitting

there in the sun
next to the med
itation pillow
on the animal
print dog mats
in the sun

we'll meditate
together
today that's
what we'll do

& then I'll
mop. I've never
mopped a floor
before

yesterday I swept
& she had never
seen that

if I wash
dishes at
night everything's
clean in
the morning

that's what
I learned
from Erin

the sun just moved
I'll never use you

in a poem
I'll use everything

& it will cover
you & the

egg crinkles
& chuckles

& the toaster
moans

it was trying
to tell me something

it was still set
to melt cheese
the egg snaps

don't forget
therapy

I forgot
I was cooking
an egg

& everything
I was so
happy

Mary made me
a pot holder

I'm fucking serious
and Honey breathes

waiting for
a taste

I'm reading Tristram
Shandy
and the Koran
and a mausoleum
of lovers

she kept
touching my foot
with her body
hint hint

I can see her
waiting feet

here have
a lick

turns out I
wasn't so hun-
gry

she's a loud eater
she grumbles &
snorts a piggy

sound; the pig

the pig is
still dying now

my grandmother
died of the Spanish

flu; she was 33

it's not really true
it was pneumonia

could you die of
the flu in 1925[1]

it was like the hummels
she carried some

soup to the sick
children across
the park & caught
it from them

oh this is pajamas
David

I almost forgot

who caught the marlin
today I've got
to ask

---

1. yes you could/ I've since/ learned

but I forgot

I sd good thank
you &

this was an ac
cess point

and
everything
else went on
the train
whined

April

wait
and rub
my leg

an old man
in a bed

a jingling
dog
stands
on all
fours

a note
book

al
most

done

Archer

There's no
elsewhere
like this

the thing
knocks
around
in the jar

and ev
eryone's
talking
it's wind

blackness
holds strings
I don't
know

what
else
holding night

by myself
I'm not
alone
though I
wish
you were
here

The Sacrament & the

Trains coming
today different
from yes
terday
there still is that
slight breeze
Maiya is the special
agent in charge
of casinos on Get
Go & not the owner
of Ozark who did not
respond to my
letter
peeing around the dumpster
peculiar slime and
cat trap
a cup of
time we get
to give
as an amend
to somebody else
not burning in

this morning
sun today
I'm starving

Painting Is the Sky

That's not a new thought
& every single thing u
Built is a perch
6 black crow
And one tiny bird
On a wire says whatever
We own the sky
And half of us
Cat our blackness
Over there
The orange & pink
& yellow where the road
Ends and it doesn't
End. Mountains
Fill the view & disappear
When night falls
What's that word
About gathering the future
It means this

April Sixteenth Twenty Twenty

Open
the window
to sun
set. Let the
light
in
that bird
that red
Elise is
40. The poverty
of my
house
is I have
no view
no mountains
and dusk
I simply
come
in having
seen all
that & I
open

the window &
it breathes
me.

My watch

is back
but I
don't
look at
it any
more

The kitten
in the
dream
is probably
dead

the writing
so cool:
Eileen
is motion

one thought
floated
to the next

swarms
of it

if I were
recording

go home
to the place

it is
possible

replaceable

one word
butter

they moved
with the
seasons

I don't
I thought

the leverage
of their
desire

could be
mine:
get out

the child
in here

wants lawns
and furniture

big window &
a dog.

books she lovers
rooms to
wander

& then
sit

Write
a lot. Throw

yr apple
in the trash

Monday Shit

I don't know if I'm knowing something or falling
apart. I put my two feet together
it's mOn day.

put the water on.

I was dropping a man off
a dark-haired friend

I was parked in the middle of the plaza

I can't stay here. I went inside a little
I gotta go
and I went up there over the lumpy hills

the store where the women
worked my friends
an old guitar
store
everything's different now cause of the pandemic
I want to go to that [I] think
can I put my bike behind the counter
or up there

no cause we're moving
I see plenty of room

next I'm all involved with them
the kids
and they're playing outside

I'm in the apartment somehow
and everyone's gone
like I woke
I coulda put my bicycle
anywhere

it's morning
I call the children like it's morning
where did this shit
come from
and I found the morning
coffee
and this is a miracle

I just called them and they came in like dogs
I dreamed this world; that's it
does it work this
way: working, dreaming

having a life, making and dying
why did I die

to dream this?

and everyone that knows me or something
somewhere or some while

I know you once in a while

I truly forgot about him
I didn't know he was
going to do that

everybody's not in a dream but
me or we find each other

here. I didn't know their fucking
names but I found their
children. I was first.

I'm waking here it's perfect
everything. Cause coffee's like

music I thought about
quitting in the future
for the better
orgasm I read that.

did it once in the 80s
we were camping and
shit and whoa

waking from that dream into
this but

my cave my hovel
afraid to put it in a suitcase
will my dreaming come

the feeling of flowing with you
but you have seven stories
and I have three
possibly three
one flooded with a baby
do I know\all I know is this
Kid.
I'm just thinking about what you're getting into
as I'm making my day
how did it end this time
feeding the yellow
dog. I was looking for a parking place
and it was my dyke
my children and I didn't know
anyone's names. Is this the story
that holds the future
or this is the day
so marvelous. Pouring some of it over & over
there I think it's perfect
and me this
prophecy right here
now it holds.

Memorial Day

cat
jumps
into
a dump
ster
shopping

May 8 – 9

IN the morning a dog
hangs out
outside
birds make
all those
sweet
sounds

my back in action
since 1949
aches

what world
I just wanted
to write
that. They are
hovering
singing
making the
day

on my
white

board
it says
radio

a collection
of shoes
from many mo
ments yes
Saturday
and the day
before

and the cold
from outside
surround
ing my
ankles too

it's 55
my phone says

I guess
I'll close
the door

the thing
that's
different

from the
poem
I wrote

forty two

years ago
I think
of myself
as a gather

er

maybe the
words are
the birds

I have
a dog

I call my
dog a
stoned
whup

she stands
at the
door

I heard her
going whup

I opened
it & looked

at her standing
there she
goes what

that's the
stoned
part

the dove's
song is
graceful
layered

hey that's maybe
where poetry
came from

and the others
barge in

some constant
tweeting

another a confirm
ing click
an agreeing rat-
tle a sweet
cheep. The

array makes
me shake
my head

it continues
around the
clock re-
pairing, group
song then

my dog barks

low grounded
thing they
think

Frama

I don't
hate
men

my back
hurts

I hate
covid

jingling
now when your

head's
in the
bowl

drinking
water

& saving
the
past

in incantations

is *this*
my thirst

Nantucket

an episode
of outta

here
in which

I have
finally

taken
the Thoreau
walk

for the new
Yorker

and all
the pilgrim
ghosts

and native
americans

are swarming
around
me like

crows.

Two Hundred Years

for Kelly

The plot
walks
by a splashing
bucket
in the hands
of a small
girl

animals
wander

naturally
dog forages

History isn't
here yet

the subject
is their
comfort
& their
needs

smoothing
crumbs

temperature
is dialogue

hello
how are
you

didn't expect
company
this late

here we
are

you got
a nice
place
here

sorry about
your husband

and your
calf

it's a terrible
thing

picking &
snacking

sound
is the storyteller

useless
people
interesting

petting a
bird

oily
cake

my warped
pen

a dog
is watching

a man watches
nothing
to do.

pull
down
the little
house

roses
and sticks

this is
a movie

the broken
house

is it
old
or new

the green

wet
water
always
new

cow got
a little
fence

like a
unicorn

and quietly
go to
sleep

to be the
target

flash of
light outside

as I'm
watching
this
our
nation's

miracle
the end.

September

I heard
a distant
girl

screaming
out there
like an
elastic

everyone
liked
the kitten
on the
boat

it's
an old
name

for a rub
ber
band

but a
band

all the same
which

is nothing
like

a tiger
that

killed
a kid

and later
the tiger

got shot

you kill

me. You

simply
kill me.

Erin

using
seasons
as yr closer

the sun
out. You
over there
belly out
book
clutched

in your
fingers
feet
draped
and a blue

stripe of
sky o–
ver your
head.

Night

crazy yale
spike out
our blue
picture
window

we're studying
here & we
are so hot

in a life of
intellection
vacation
celebration

I love you so
much

9/19/19

Pink Margot (2020)

The crouching businessman is not sitting
with his love in the landscape
or alone on the fire-escape
with his red hair. I see three yellow
buildings in a dark night
I see a back turned to
me this year and I am sad.

Why do I like buildings

and fire the final painting,
is.

I am not in this show &
when I counted horses
I landed right
here

where horses begin. The problem with eternity
there's no way to see everything

in a pink painting

I miss Margot
but not all at once

I miss her again

pencil & pen

A minute is so
long
on my birthday
snow feasts
on the open
air and she
bought me flowers
in my color
which is
orange
my color is orange
you don't know
your color is
orange. I do
but it is such
a gift
Myra had snow
I said
I want that
and now it
has come
71 is a birthday
of tiny

gifts
crafts and tinkers
just like
this

Love with you
was messy &
brite

I don't mean
forever
I mean

last night.
Accidental
pawing. Creatures
with new
& shaggy
bodies
in a hollow
of lowering
shade

Time had
us in
its nest. You

will always
be the
best.

X

The center
of the
universe
is here
& I continue
to read
things
about millions
of stars
about ice chips
along the
outer rim
of the solar
system
and the
names
of moons
this year
this year
that extends
along the
movements
of the sky
our crooked

earth &
our crooked–
er sun
the star
that <u>isn't</u>
in the constel-
lation of
the swan. Because
we are living
in a grey
area now
there's no
reason to
assume
that August
one when
Saturn &
Jupiter
have their
last kiss
will have
any thing
to do with
you or us.
And the
fact that
I never
really needed
you enough

will not
be so impor-
tant. I
look up
in the
sky outside
of your
house
I have no
way to
read this
endless
black
turning
thing over
my head
that I
have always
loved.

The nothing
spot
where
a tree's
so long
ago been.

Beloved Park

for Carlina Rivera

The city
is like
a mismanaged
notebook
found
on a bench
by a hope
ful man
who spun
a tale
for the city
that wanted
to change
but once
the notebook
was his
he began
tearing out &
selling
its pages.
One page
the park

we
love
sold to a
man
who insisted
he could
make
the park
a boat.
But where
will the trees
go we
cried and the
birds that
are living
in them. The
park sailed
away in that
man's
dream. It's
the corruption
of govern
ment. It was
my bench
it was
our page
this
is our
sunny
day.

The Park

Politicians
are like actors
and real
estate invest
ment
groups
are like vampires
politicians
think they
have to
let bite
them or
they won't get
any work.
The rest of
us are humans
living around
the show.
Squirrels
are squirrels
birds are
birds. Our
park is a
giant stage

we thought
was real
because we
walked there
everyday. It
is a set
that Robert
Moses
built so
that he
could run
his high
way longside
it. My dog
knows the
story, you
know the
story everyone
knows
the story
the vampires
are building
a giant
boat on top
of our
park in order
to save
it. It will
take them

about
ten years
the waters
will rise.
the children
will be
old. I
will be
dead. The
vampires
will be
rich. The politicians
will have
these tiny
vials
of blood
all lined up
on their
shelves
from the years
they were
in that
play.

Home In Our Time

I thought
I heard
cows moaning
but it was
my dog's
breathing.
My cold
feet
I got
the
shot
she asks
him
if he
warmed
the blood
as if
it were
milk
and she
was his
kid

and he
did.

Bill
Compton
has Bill
Clinton's
voice.
you must
have no
ticed
this. His
sweater
is not
black
it's burgun
dy
the colour
of blood
floating
through
a tube.

I sold
mine at
a storefront
near
the strand

in the
seventies
on a fake
leather
couch
I lied
near
a man
who was
a regular.
They told
me to
keep
pumping
my hands
I nearly
passed
out to see
my outsides
passing
through
a tube.

I was
told
to never
come back.
And

now I
am a
vampire.
How
is that
true.

Held

I forgot
the distant pink
behind
the trees
I was heading
to the super
market
I would
get it later
somehow
in the parking
lot per
haps on my
phone
My butt on
the boat
and the
pink
comes
back
in memory.

Look What the Cat Dragged in

Sometimes
I feel
like I'm
in
some movie
about
death

this rainy night
pull

your hood
off and
get inside

the eerie
splashing
silence of it.
Each
eerie
step.

No I do not
want

to get
on your
bus
unlocking

my bike

I thought about
them tonight

I could
try

go on a journey
see everyone

no one does
that any
more

and then we
were all
in the room
the zoom

room &
that's why
I was

thinking
of them
because

they were
there

I don't
know
them at all
I could
make
the effort

I'd be
known
as them
that
came
that one
time

the whole
city
gleaming in
my head
wet &

black
I'm out

in it
with
my groceries

I don't even
want you
now

I've got
to say

this. She
showed

up late &

I thought
look what

the cat
dragged
in. It

meant
we were
close

and there
they were

in my
head

that's where
they live

feeding
me
things

look what
the cat
dragged
in. Would
she know
it was
love

would anyone?

Two Things

April 9
It's Ireland first & that's why I
must read Anna Burns's
Milkman before Gillian Rose

the ruby
pajamas

that I
bought
in Cavin

the rocky
place

my family
came
from
and that's
why they
drank

it was
cozy &
then
it seemed
sad to

wear
pajamas
bottom
and top

ruby
or maroon
dark
red

so I
got
rid of
the top

and felt
a little
freer

more tossed
when
I slept

but I
came a
round

eventually
to wanting

the whole
thing

not fancy
at all

not sad
I bought
em in
a men's
shop

the guy
was re
spectful &

offered
a small

it's the
absolute
fucking
fact &

tonight
by complete
accident
I'm wearing
a ruby

teeshirt

one of
my favorite

I was
wearing
black earlier
everyone
was. It
was dark
in the
rain

so when I
got home
I put
on this different
shirt
& I
felt
honestly
forced
by these

conditions

the red
teeshirt &

the dark
maroon
pajama
bottoms
from
Ireland

to keep
to myself
here
where
it's al
right

in all this
dark red
tonight

& I remember
all the
bright

smiling
we were doing
on the
phone
earlier
today
and I
liked

it so much

I mean
this
is another
subject

but sometimes
you just
have to
work.

Can I get
away
with any
thing

alone in
bed
and my
clothes
match.

And I

cont'd
to this.
it's nice
around
here. We've
got this

and that.

Did I
get this
cause
it's cold

it'd
be over
fast

I don't know
what they
expect
me to think
of with
these little green

crowns
mixed in
w the food.

It's supposed
to be nice
like greens
in with
the flowers
but these
are not
flowers

these are fish
dead

not for too
long I
hope &
they swam
past
green
things in
their
youth
yesterday.

I'm well
aware

of the horror
of the
world
the silence
is not
worse

I'm thinking
of her
all of a
sudden
with this
chewy
fish
in my mouth
in a way
it must
be terrible
to win
now.

She is the
cherry

of everyone's
defeat

she is the
cherry

mysteriously
I ate
the old
fish

and she
is the

cherry

salut

I kept the
mask

on cause
I thought
I looked good

this restaurant
really needs
a candle

& like it heard
me a plane
passed overhead.

Diet Coke

says recycle
me

I took the
dog
on the sub
way
today

And today
I have
an alarm

on my phone

called Joan
Mitchell.

And later
on tonight
I said
I'd be
Joaning

This dog
sees

everything
on 2nd
Ave

not far
historical
ly from
where
Robert Harms
met Joan
Mitchell
in the apt
of Joe
LeSueur
right
over
there

I think of build
ings
collapsing

I'm having
a slice
nearby

at the party
everyone's
laughing

I say
I'm boning
Joan
tonight

I'm boning
up on
Joan
Mitchell

for the
famous
woman
artist
podcast

Honey
badly wants
a bite

the light
just changed

it's bright

the kind of
Stéphane
Grappelli
violin
playing

while bicycles
pass

Matthew
said
I would
have sobbed
the end
was so
good

if I
had

authentic
feelings

we laugh

I just
spent
an hour

zooming
with my
shrink

the parade
of exes

in Province
town

the man
in the
orange

cap
walking

away

I would
cry if
I wasn't

so damn
joyous

he's lowering
the awning
on the
pizza
shop

but these
feelings
just won't

go
away.

Mice

they see
a cluster
of small
rubber

ducks &
scraps of
broken
shells

& think

I'll shit
there

we describe
them as
brazen
when they
run
through
what
actually

is their
home

so I
begin

to kill
them

because
I'm better
than
them
one was
seen
running
into
the bathroom
my bathroom

& a small
frail
one
was found
dead
right

on the
floor &

the poison

is working

& I feel
bad

because
in fact
I like
living

with them.

They're
part
of my
life

their
little
shits

every
where &

I have
killed
their
child

they're
unclean
anyone
would
say

isn't it
why I
must kill
them

but I'm
unclean
too

isn't
that why
they're
here

and I
generally
have guests
who say

this place
is so
small
they look

around &
I feel
shame

& I look
around
usually right
after a
trip

or in a
couple
of days &
it's small

but not
to them

they think
it's huge

perfect

and that is
a friend

& why don't
I keep
them

around

come back
come back

& I know
you <u>will</u>

the rape raggedy tiara

home which
is a ham
burger
a dog lit
erally
sees your
meal &
licks
their
lips

I had
a moment
of joy
on the
subway
after
I
went to the
eye doctor
I'm either
there
or not
in terms

of greatness
blow your
horn

he was good

and the
little bag
of grapes
wrapped
in paper
a nice
little pouch

I bought
on a
whim
I ate
them so
fast do
you do
that
there's something
about
the sweetness
of grapes
I almost
choke
dirty grapes

fast like
secret
sex
the best
nobody
knew about
that. My
own

the little pig
is dirty
on my
computer
it
was a
joke
I had
with you
or something
I got
from you
but you
didn't
get, the
holes
& the stones

she didn't
even notice

her daughter
was raped
what was
she dead
then not
now
the endlessly
alive
mother
the one in
charge
of anti
social
media
is losing
hers &
she's awful
to everyone
but
her crew
refuses
to mention
it. Being
loyal
to her loss.
But I
am loyal
to the loss
of the

present
the only
loss
worth
noting. I should
charge
you by the
minute
you pain
in the
ass. She's
going
she's
going
she's
gone. It's
winter &
I'm
cooking vegetables
with
you that's
what I
miss &
giving you
holidays
like
a child.
The cowboy
rode

on Christmas

the rape
raggedy
tiara
everyone
goes. No
one
is a king.

for Alex Katz

Because
these
paintings
are both
coming &
going
finding
nature &
losing
it I
feel silent
but that
isn't
how you
feel. Waiting
world
violent
friend.

Eva, After Getting Off the Boat

I'm something
unreliable
and this
is a day for
poetry.

My body
one big
explosion

or rev
elation
or crinkly
thing.

I go back.
These
threads
of paper
that hap
pen to be
my econ
omy:

repeatable
& manifold

serial &
sundry. What
is Eileen
talking a
bout. I got
myself

ready to fly
with a
thin layer
of literal
ly sleep

but what
we mean
by cons
ciousness
is it
writing?
This? But
what?   I

go on

carrying
hordes

awaiting
an opportun
ity. I cut
it in
half being
careful
to say

thank you &
wander
on. I'll make
something

public
eventually
filtering
back to the
real, a

promise
or two. And
    really

keeping
some
room
for the lively
impertinence
of change.

I'm a little
unsure
if you
believe
in that. Do I.
I get
up.

I bump
my head
on something
soft. A per
son. Sor–
ry. It's o
kay.

Is this 18 or 19.
His fin
gers
flex

now he's
explaining
the equip
ment
to his neigh
bor. Neigh–
bor? Somebody
somewhere

This float–
y stuff

knowledge
the faces
coming at
me: hopeful
suspicious
surly bland
they just
want
wanting
   now
I am travelling.
What if
I really
was ev
eryone. Forget
all the
neighbor
shit. Does
this have
neighbors
how does it
hold what it's
writing
writing
by hand. I love
this edge.

It wasn't
even a
neigh
borhood Bob
& I de
cided
to spend
my life

there

    least
our row
is complete.
The plane
has too
many people
the world
has. Series
of cartoons
in which

the world
has sad
thoughts:
I'm dead.
But who
may read

my signs.
I killed
the dinosaurs
and now
I kill
you. Is
any body
out there.

A planet
hope
lessly
alone. Calling
to the
present &
the past.
The old def

ignition
got us
here.
     My

black
ness is
a sword

jabbing
through

space
lacking a tar
get you
did this
to your
self the only
bands
are marching
bands

I'm part
of one

night
a serial
prayer
this is volume
well how
do I count.
I only
have voice

sound &
a good pen.
Our ex
changes
of warmth
can't be
traded

in for
a fortune. This
is the future.
My white
friend
said
I look
good. You
brought
me here
to advo
cate for
him

the best
thing
I've ever
seen
a mirror
of way
too late
don't we
need
to see
ourselves
a lonely
earth
burning
up with

a party
hat & a drink
in his hand
as if
making
a lot of
noise
was a plan.
If I play
nothing
and see
what it
has. If

I don't
wear gloves
see how
my hands
do covered
with spots
& bulging
nerves
there's some
thing im
possibly
true about
the body
anyone's

I am
still
in Greece
and Laura's
women
wrinkles or no
            are
weaving. It's
just that
wanting

to produce

only
that hum
ming, the
car went

whop
whop

what if
what I
do now
killed
the dino
saurs

I be
trayed
you so long
ago &
you

hear that
sound

What's that
unpacked
the mar
velous

is someone
spent lying
on the
beach
looking at
its feet.

If most
of the people
of the
people
on the
planet
are lost

but you
see this
big blue
orb so
far you
can't even
hear

them
cry
I need
a nap. She's
a recording
he's laughing
at work
on a plane
it's usually
him mar
ried
with kids
dick
firing in the
future

you don't
picture
your kids
in those
human
forms

let's play
a game
and tell
me where
you hid
it on
my planet

just a
little bit
of change
I feel
lost

and
more com
mingled
with
all those
people

crying in
jail

dirty
lost
a hand lost
an arm

I was
just go
ing

to a fuck
ing wed
ding

how dare
I plan

for there
to be
a future
strap
in to the
plane.

When we take
off it
will change
your thought.

He made
art out
of very
strong
light. The cor
porate

light
of the present
& the
future. As
a woman

she would
obviously
be more
concerned
with

organizing
loss

but it's a little
bit later

just as
dark
out there

where we
spin.
What
if someone

was reading
this
is a book

a world
in which
they killed

everyone
but pre
tended

it was
not
happening.

It is

and she puts
the broken
parts
the lights
fading
in Greece. In
a gallery
in Athens
This morning
she crosses
her legs &
reads the
screen

on her
lap which
is glowing.
I transport
the apparatus
for the cel
ebratory

Cake. Don't
bitch
I thought &
I'm driving
her home &
her daughter

is smiling
holding
their
child from
another
part
of the
planet.
James,
she made
a home
for him. The
home
everywhere

this is
what

I think
is good
do care &
offer
band aids
and see
the hurt &
dig in
their purse
on the
boat
to help.
I am grateful
that you
have seen.

have I
seen
anyone in
their
pain
my mother
scarcely
breathing
we waiting
her out.

They don't
care cause
I never
cld. But I
care
where.

standing way
outside
seeing the blue
which is
only in
here & I'm
finishing
cause there's
nothing else
to do. I got
the part
where you
don't

say. You
just do. All of
her face
is gleaming
at me

The image
is fixed.

When
she moves
be kind.

We are

all engaging

in the mystery

of what
we have

done with
our kind

we are
hurling

something's

going
on & it's

comforting
to not
entirely
be the
last but
being one

of them

the painless
world
cause

you're so
far

get close
it's your
only

one &
you
can really
feel

it &
hear
it. The

turning is
crying

the light
what
is it
made

of is
dim,

breathe
present

change.

Acknowledgments

I wanted to say *a "Working Life"* means the poems are the plan, not that this book is about labor exactly.

Some of these guys appeared in *Poetry, Journal Nine, Adjacent Pineapple, Columbia, Paris Review, The Trip, The Recluse, Gulf Coast, New Yorker, Ambit, Nectar Feed* broadside series, *Harper's*, HOUSE PARTY #2, Academy of American Poets' Poem-a-Day series, canwehaveourballback.org, *Diaphanes: Punk Philology, Big Bend Sentinel*, Jason Dodge's fivehundred-places.com/about, *Artforum, New Republic, Together in a Sudden Strangeness: America's Poets Respond to the Pandemic, Textur #2* (Kelly Reichardt/Viennale), *The Atlantic*, and *Truant*.

"The Library" was commissioned by the fact that someone won a dog poem from me in an auction to benefit PS New York in 2019. I met their newfies and took a walk with them in Chelsea and the poem is the result.

"Casper" is the final monologue by a puppet of the same name at the end of *The Trip*, a super-eight puppet road film I made with David Fenster in 2018. It's on YouTube.

And now I want to thank who I always thank, a big one to Emily Burns at Grove and Peter Blackstock for liking poetry so much and always PJ Mark and especially this time Will Farris who sat with me one afternoon and helped me make a list of poems that would make a book if there was one. This is that, thanks Will.

And Ama Birch for a late and valuable read.

Also want to thank Piergiorgio Pepe and Iordanis Kerenidis who made Phenomenon 2 on the island of Anafi, and even helped bring some of this work to Antipodes and Krystalli Glyniadakis who brought these poems into Greek. And Jason Dodge who was there and Quinn Lattimer and Iris Touliatou and Eva Barto who all inspired so much of this work. Joan Mitchell was probably also in the room and always Robert Harms and I'm grateful to the pandemic for causing me to write poems like it was the '70s and to my orange pitbull and friend, Honey, who was with me all that time.